13 Art Techniques
Children Should Know

Angela Wenzel

PRESTEL

Munich · London · New York

Contents

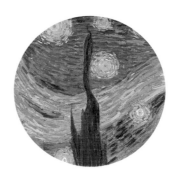

This book introduces you to thirteen important artistic techniques and shows you how they're used. Specific works of art illustrate why artists choose particular techniques and show just how closely the technique is related to what the work communicates.

A glossary at the end of the book explains terms that might be difficult to understand. These terms are marked in the text with an asterisk (*). At the beginning of each chapter, a timeline helps you to place a technique within its historical context. Questions that make you stop and think or test your knowledge are scattered throughout the book. Their answers can be found on page 46.

If you want to learn more about a specific technique, check out our tips about books to read or museums to visit. And last but not least, you'll almost certainly want to try out some of the techniques yourself: take a look at our suggestions for do-it-yourself projects.

Have fun exploring!

Name:
  drawing
Material:
  charcoal, graphite,*
  red chalk, chalk, India
  ink on stone, wood,
  parchment, paper,
  canvas
Tools:
  sticks, fingers,
  pencils, pens, brushes
Some Artists:
  Stone Age people,
  Albrecht Dürer,
  Leonardo da Vinci,
  Adolph von Menzel

A Line a Day

As long ago as the Stone Age, people had mastered the art of drawing. They used sharp tools to scratch pictures into stone and decorated the walls of caves with charred wood, colorful soil, and brightly colored rocks.

Drawing—the art of the line—is a very ancient technique. An individual artist's particular style or "handwriting" can be seen clearly in a drawing. Anything that can make a line can be used for drawing. Each material has its own special qualities.

Today the pencil is the best-known drawing tool. Pencil "lead" is actually made of graphite,* but people originally mistook this heavy, shiny metal for lead ore.* To manufacture graphite pencil cores, graphite powder is mixed with clay to harden and bind it. Then the mixture is fired in an oven. The more clay, the harder the finished core is.

Second Chinese Horse,
Unknown artist, cave painting, c. 17,000 B.C., Caves of Lascaux, Dordogne

Prehistoric* artists most often made pictures with animals, but they also drew human figures and abstract* forms. In 1940 teenagers accidentally stumbled upon the cave drawings in Lascaux, in southern France.

Tip
Drawings by Stone Age people have also been found in the caves of Altamira in Spain. The Deutsches Museum in Munich contains reproductions of these cave drawings. For pictures of the reproductions, see http://www.deutsches-museum.de/en/exhibitions/materials-production/altamira-cave/

around 1300 Paper first used for drawings

1492 Christopher Columbus discovers the New World

around 1500 Pencils made with graphite* are in use in England

1795 Pencils with a graphite-clay core appear in Paris

around 1900 German factories in Nuremberg and Fuerth produce around 225 million pencils

1940 Discovery of cave paintings in Lascaux

| 1000 | 1100 | 1200 | 1300 | 1400 | 1500 | 1600 | 1700 | 1800 | 1900 | 2000 | A.D. 2100 |

Self-Portrait as a Thirteen-Year-Old, Albrecht Dürer, silverpoint drawing, 1484, Graphische Sammlung, Vienna

It was a bold act by the young Albrecht Dürer to draw himself in front of a mirror: with silverpoint it's not possible to erase mistakes. This technique produces only very fine lines, made by using a lot of pressure. Each stroke must be just right. Here, the young artist used hatching* for the dark areas, including the shadows in the folds of cloth and in the face.

Test your knowledge: Why wasn't the silverpoint stylus made entirely of silver?
(Solution on page 46)

Fishing Boats at Sea,
Vincent van Gogh, 1888,
reed pen, Musées Royaux
des Beaux Arts, Brussels

Pen and ink are good for drawing contours, or lines that reveal the shapes of natural forms. Van Gogh's strokes appear to have been made quickly; they are vigorous and filled with movement.

Drawing charcoal,

Charcoal is one of the oldest drawing materials. Most of the cave drawings at Altamira and Lascaux were made with iron oxide,* sanguine (red chalk), and charcoal. Hard drawing charcoal is made by burning wood chips from wooden boards, soft charcoal by burning thin twigs. The tip can be used to draw lines and the broad side can be used to darken entire surfaces. Charcoal can be wiped to a gray tone, but it is also easily smudged. A fixative* can be used to preserve charcoal drawings.

Artists of the Renaissance* often drew with a rodlike metal utensil called a stylus, which was made of lead, copper, or bronze and had a rounded silver tip. Their technique was called silverpoint. Since hard metals do not leave a trace on normal paper, the drawing surface had to be prepared with chalk or gesso.* This process made the surface slightly bumpy, enabling it to catch and hold fine silver lines produced from the stylus. Over time, these lines darkened and turned brown.

Pen and ink are especially good for loose and fluid drawings. Ink pens can be made of plants (including reed and bamboo), quills (feathers from a goose or swan), or metal. Reeds and quills are cut diagonally and the tip is split. The long shaft is moistened with ink. Firm pressure on the pen creates thick lines and soft pressure creates finer ones.

Self-Portrait,
Leonardo da Vinci,
red chalk on paper,
c. 1515–16, Biblioteca
Reale, Turin

Sanguine, or red chalk, is a kind of earth pigment containing red iron oxides.* It has been used by people since prehistoric cave-dwelling times. Lumps of sanguine are prepared by being broken into pieces or by being ground into a powder, mixed into a paste, and then pressed into sticks.

The Angelic Salutation*,
Veit Stoss, 1517–18,
limewood, polychrome,
St. Lorenz, Nuremberg

Each kind of wood has
its own special qualities.
Wood from the large-leafed
linden tree, which German
artist Veit Stoss used for his
sculptures, grows relatively
quickly, has uniform fibers,
and is soft, light, and elas-
tic. These qualities make it
easy to carve. The sculpture
shown here is polychrome,
which means it has been
painted in colors. Its figures
are over nine feet high:
taller than any real person!

Veit Stoss 1447–1533

Michelangelo Buonarroti 1475–1564

1939–1945 Second World War

Auguste Rodin 1840–1917
Constantin Brancusi 1876 – 1957

around 100 B.C. Venus de Milo

1914–1918 First World War

| 00 B.C. | A.D. 1000 | 1100 | 1200 | 1300 | 1400 | 1500 | 1600 | 1700 | 1800 | 1900 | 2000 |

Hew, Carve, and Chisel

When asked how he was able to create the figure of David from a block of marble, Michelangelo is said to have answered, "David is already inside. I simply have to cut away everything that's hiding him."

It is written that the Italian artist personally selected his marble blocks from the famous stone quarry of Carrara before they were cut. The Latin verb *sculpere* means to fashion by sculpting, to carve, or to chisel. There are two basic kinds of sculpture: carving and modeling. In carving, the artist removes material and has to pay attention to the inner structure of the stone or wood.

To keep it from splitting, wood needs to be well seasoned (or dried) before being carved. And since humidity can weaken the wood over time and make it more likely to split, the sculptor has to understand where the weak points in the wood are before beginning to carve. Another way sculptors prevent splitting is by cutting out the heartwood, or the hard inner part of the wood. This is why most figures carved from wood are hollow inside.

Name:
  carving, sculpting
Material:
  wood, marble, sandstone
Tools:
  knife, gouge, hammer, chisel, grinding and polishing tools
Some Artists:
  Veit Stoss, Tilman Riemenschneider, Michelangelo, Auguste Rodin, Constantin Brancusi

Unfinished Slave,
 around 1520–23, marble, Galleria dell' Accademia, Florence

This slave really looks like he's been inside the marble all along and is struggling to free himself. Art historians disagree about whether Michelangelo intentionally left the sculpture unfinished or not.

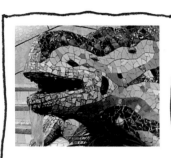

Name:
  mosaic
Material:
  pebbles, colored
  glass tiles, mother
  of pearl and semi-
  precious stones, glass
  and porcelain shards
Some Artists:
  Sumerians,* ancient
  Greeks and Romans,
  Byzantines,* Antoni
  Gaudí, Simon Rodia,
  Niki de St. Phalle

Bench,
Antoni Gaudí, 1900 –14,
Parco Güell, Barcelona

The Spanish architect
Antoni Gaudí created
brightly colored
mosaics of ceramic,
porcelain, and
shards of glass.

Tessera by Tessera

Mosaics are pictures or ornaments* composed of tiny colored objects. Scholars are unsure about whether the term "mosaic" comes from a Greek word referring to the Muses* or the Arabic word *musanik*, which means "decorated."

Around 3000 B.C. the Sumerians* were already decorating the walls of their temples with cone mosaics, which they made by attaching clay cones with colored tips onto a stone surface. The ancient Greeks used mosaics made of colored pebbles as flooring. Glass mosaics are able to produce the most delicate and brilliant color effects. The liquid glass is pressed into a flat slab, which is then cut into small tiles when it has cooled. Silver and gold mosaics are made by melting silver or gold leaf* between two sheets of glass.

Mosaic tiles, called tesserae, are either placed directly into the wet plaster or assembled indirectly. The "indirect" method involves many steps. First, a full scale copy of the artist's drawing is transferred onto cardboard. The drawing is then copied section by section onto transparent paper, and the tesserae are attached to the paper upside down. Next, the sections of paper with the attached tesserae are attached to the wall in their proper places one at a time. Finally, the gaps between the tesserae are filled in with cement-like material called grout.

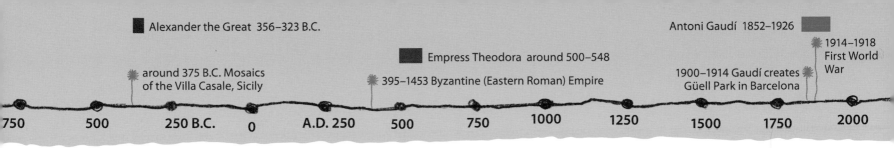

Alexander the Great 356–323 B.C.

Antoni Gaudí 1852–1926

Empress Theodora around 500–548

1914–1918
First World
War

around 375 B.C. Mosaics
of the Villa Casale, Sicily

395–1453 Byzantine (Eastern Roman) Empire

1900–1914 Gaudí creates
Güell Park in Barcelona

| 750 | 500 | 250 B.C. | 0 | A.D. 250 | 500 | 750 | 1000 | 1250 | 1500 | 1750 | 2000 |

Activity

Look for pebbles of various colors and assemble them into a mosaic.
You can find instructions for making a mosaic on paper in the book *Art in Action* by Maja Pitamic, 2010.

Tip
Sumerian* cone mosaics from around 3300–3100 B.C. can be seen at the Metropolitan Museum of Art in New York. You can also see a picture of these mosaics at http://www.metmuseum.org/toah/works-of-art/L.1995.48.2.

Empress Theodora and Her Attendants,
Unknown artist, around A.D. 547, Church of San Vitale, Ravenna

Shimmering tiles called tesserae were the ideal material for depicting this Byzantine* empress. The tesserae in her crown are made of mother-of-pearl, a gleaming white substance created from shells.

11

Name:
　fresco
Material:
　lime, sand, water,
　pigments*
Tools:
　trowel, heavy paper,
　needle, charcoal,
　animal hair brush,
　soft bristle brush
Some Artists:
　Giotto di Bondone,
　Andrea Mantegna,
　Raphael, Michel-
　angelo, Giovanni
　Battista Tiepolo

**The Founding
of Rome (detail),**
Gentile da Fabriano,
1411–12, Loggia Palazzo
Trinci, Foligno

During antiquity and the
middle ages in Europe,
fresco painters made
underdrawings with
earth colors containing
red iron oxide.* These
drawings are called sin-
opia.* They can be seen
here only because the
layer of plaster with the
painting has partially
chipped away.

All Along the Wall

Fresco painting is not for the timid! As the name implies,
he who hesitates is lost …

The Italians call it "dipingere a fresco," which literally means "painting fresh." This name refers to the plaster on the wall made of lime and
sand, which is painted while still wet. But although fresco artists have to
work very fast once the plaster is wet, the preparations beforehand are
extremely time-consuming. First, the outlines of the artist's drawing
(or "cartoon") have to be transferred onto a large piece of thick paper,
and then tiny holes are pricked along the lines.

To make a fresco, a layer of fine plaster is spread on the wall over the rough
underlayer. But the artist has to be careful to apply only as much plaster
as can be painted while still wet. The artist then cuts out the correspond-
ing section of the cartoon, attaches it to the wall, and taps a bag of soot
over the holes to transfer the drawing onto the wall.

Giotto di Bondone 1266–1337

Gentile da Fabriano around 1370–1427

July 27, 1944 Allied* artillery attack at Pisa

Giovanni Battista Tiepolo 1696–1760

1939–1945 Second World War

900   1000   1100   1200   1300   1400   1500   1600   1700   1800   1900   2000

Frescos in the Cappella degli Scrovegni (Arena Chapel),
Giotto di Bondone, 1304–06, Padua

Italian artist Giotto painted more than a hundred scenes from the Bible in the Arena Chapel. Assistants mixed the paint for him from earth colors and real lapis lazuli.* Giotto also painted "a secco"—that is, after the plaster was already dry. The plaster would be moistened and the color applied with limewash.*

Tip
Many sinopia* are on exhibit in the Museo delle Sinopie in Pisa, Italy. Numerous frescos in Pisa were damaged during the Second World War and their underdrawings revealed. You can see some of the museum's sinopia at http://www.stilepisano.it/immagini/Pisa_museo_delle_sinopie.htm

Pigment* mixed with water is used for painting thin glazes,* while lime-washes* are used to create a thicker layer of color. A fresco is made section by section. Sometimes the seams that separate one "day's work" from another can be seen quite clearly. The colors become permanently fixed in the plaster.

The Great Wave off Kanagawa, Katsushika Hokusai,
around 1830, colored woodcut

Japanese artist Hokusai drew this design, but cutters and printers
executed the print. To make a colored woodcut, several blocks must be
printed together, one for each color. For the snow cloud above Mt. Fuji,
the printer painted the gradually changing shades of dark and light
gray directly onto a single block.

Albrecht Dürer 1471–1528

Rembrandt van Rijn 1606–1666

Beginning of the 1600s Modern copper plate etching technique developed
1517 Martin Luther criticizes the Catholic Church in his *Ninety-Five Theses*

Katsushika Hokusai 1760–1849
Franz Marc 1880–1916

1618–1648
Thirty Years' War

1513 First iron plate etching

1914–1918 First World War

| 1000 | 1100 | 1200 | 1300 | 1400 | 1500 | 1600 | 1700 | 1800 | 1900 | 2000 | 2100 |

Art Off the Press

Have you ever walked into your home and noticed how your dirty shoes left conspicuous marks on the clean floor? You had just made a print with your shoe soles!

The artistic technique of relief printmaking, such as a woodcut, functions in a similar way. First, the artist makes a preliminary drawing on a wooden board, bearing in mind that the image will be reversed when it is printed. All of the portions that will remain white in the final image are cut away from the board with a knife or chisel. Ink is then applied to the raised portions of the finished woodblock, a moistened sheet of paper is laid on top, and the paper is rubbed with the balls of the hands. Printing presses, such as the standing press,* produce a more evenly detailed print.

Name:
    printing / woodcut
Material:
    wood (pear, cherry, boxwood), water-colors or oil paints, smooth paper, Japanese paper (washi)*
Tools:
    gouge, crowbar, flat-bladed chisel
Some Artists:
    Katsushika Hokusai, Franz Marc, Ernst Ludwig Kirchner

Tiger,
Franz Marc, 1912, woodcut

Woodcut makes it possible for an artist to play in interesting ways with black and white. In some places the lines appear black—or positive—on a white ground, and in others they appear white—or negative—on a black ground. The black portions of the print always indicate the parts of the wooden block that the cutter has not cut away.

Name:
   printing / etching
Material:
   metal (copper, zinc),
   intaglio inks, laid
   paper,* Japanese
   paper (washi)*
   Tools: etching needle
Tools:
   etching needle
Some Artists:
   Albrecht Dürer,
   Rembrandt van Rijn,
   Max Klinger, Edgar
   Degas, Pablo Picasso

In intaglio printmaking, the lines to be printed lie below the surface of the plate. One kind of intaglio technique is etching. Drypoint is a type of etching in which the artist etches the lines directly into a copper or zinc plate, which requires a great deal of strength. Another method is to cover the plate with a material that resists being destroyed by acid. An artist can then lightly and easily draw a picture onto this surface with an etching needle. Next, the plate is submerged in an acid that "bites" the lines into the plate. The printer then covers the entire finished plate with ink, wiping the ink away from the flat parts so that it remains only in the etched lines. Finally, the plate is printed in a high-pressure printing press where, together with the sheet of paper and a felt pad, the plate is run through two cylinders turning in opposite directions. This pressure causes the paper to absorb the ink from the etched lines.

Prints are original works of art and not copies. It is easy to tell a real woodcut by looking at the reverse of the sheet, where the printed portions are slightly raised. An original etching can be identified by the impressions the edge of the plate has made in the paper.

Old Woman Sleeping,
Rembrandt van Rijn,
c. 1635, etching

Dutch artist Rembrandt
loved the drypoint
technique. He was
as talented with the
drypoint needle as he
was with a drawing
pencil.

**Saint Jerome
in His Study,**
Albrecht Dürer,
engraving,1514

Another kind of intaglio printmaking is engraving. To make an engraving, the artist uses a burin (or small chisel) to cut very fine lines, either parallel or crosshatched*, into a polished copper plate. The shavings produced by the cutting have to be removed with a scraper. If you look at the lines through a magnifying glass, you can see how they begin as fine as a hair, thicken, and then taper off again. This master engraving by Albrecht Dürer shows Jerome, an ancient Christian priest and saint, at his writing desk in the background. A large lion can be seen in the foreground: an unusual pet! According to legend, Jerome gained the lion's friendship after removing a thorn from its paw.

✳ From the A.D. 800s Watercolor painting with glazes*

850　　900　　950　　1000　　1050　　1100　　1150　　1200　　1250　　1300　　1350　　1400

Name:
　watercolor
Material:
　watercolor paints
　on rough or smooth
　sized watercolor
　paper, Japanese
　paper (washi),*
　parchment/vellum*
Tools:
　sable hair or
　synthetic hair brush
　with a fine point
Some Artists:
　William Turner, Paul
　Cézanne, Paul Klee,
　Emil Nolde, Maria
　Sybilla Merian

In Glowing Color

Watercolor painting is among the most difficult painting techniques. Nothing reveals true mastery like watercolor.

As the name implies, watercolor paints are soluble (or turn to liquid) in water. They consist of very finely ground pigments* and gum arabic* as a binder.* They can be purchased in tubes or pans.

Watercolors are not opaque, which means you can see the "support" (the paper or other painting surface) through the paint. This quality makes corrections almost impossible, but it also makes the colors especially luminous. If they are applied in thin glazes,* watercolors are delicate and airy, but their brilliant colors can also seem to glow dramatically.

The color white is missing from the watercolor palette. In watercolor, white is made by leaving the paper support free of paint. Variations in brightness are obtained by applying more or less paint. The watercolorist can mix colors not only on the palette but also by layering different colors directly on the paper. Special and unpredictable effects can be achieved when the artist uses wet paint on wet paper: this is known as "wet in wet" technique

Venice: A Storm,
Joseph Mallord William Turner, undated, watercolor, British Museum, London

British artist Turner drew the city with a fine brush. Then he placed the clouds, fog, and rain over it. The clouds you see towards the top, painted wet in wet, flow into one another.

471–1528

Maria Sibylla Merian 1647–1717

Paul Cézanne 1839–1906

Paul Klee 1879–1940

Joseph Mallord William Turner 1775–1851

Emil Nolde 1867–1956

1620 English settlers arrive in North America on the Mayflower ship

Franco-Prussian War 1870–1871

1914–1918 First World War

| 1450 | 1500 | 1550 | 1600 | 1650 | 1700 | 1750 | 1800 | 1850 | 1900 | 1950 | 2000 |

1925 e. 2. (E3wi) – Die Flora der Heide

The Flora of the Heath, Paul Klee, 1925, watercolor, Staatliche Graphische Sammlung (State Collection of Graphic Art), Munich

German-Swiss artist Paul Klee painted the upper quarter of this picture, which looks like the sky, wet in wet. There, the edges of the painted stripes run together. But with the squares, triangles, and circles, he waited until each layer was dry and only at the very end did he add the dots on top.

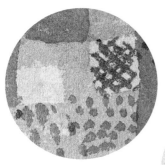

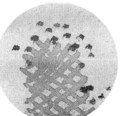

Can you guess which colors Klee combined here?

You can easily make watercolors from plants. With the help of an adult, try simmering onion skins, red beets, rose hips, dandelion leaves, or another plant you like in water for 15 to 30 minutes. The color from the plant will seep into the water, producing a lovely broth. Once the broth has cooled, you can use it to create your watercolor masterpiece!

Further reading: If you'd like to make pictures like Paul Klee, check out *Paul Klee for Children* by Silke Vry, 2011.

Leonardo da Vinci 1452–1519

From the 1200s
Oil painting is known

1400s *Strasburg Manuscript*
(the earliest known handbook
of painting techniques)

1110 1150 1190 1230 1270 1310 1350 1390 1430 1470 1510 1550

The Arnolfini Portrait,
Jan van Eyck, 1434, oil on
wood, National Gallery,
London

This oil painting was
made in Bruges, Flanders
(in what is now Belgium)
for the wedding of
Giovanni Arnolfini, a
wealthy Italian merchant,
and Giovanna Cenami.
It is filled with details
that can only be seen
on closer examination.
Of special interest is the
round, bulging mirror in
the background, which
expands the viewing
angle. Flemish artist Jan
van Eyck used this trick
to show us the ceiling
beams and the witnesses
to the wedding cere-
mony, who were standing
in the doorway.

Vincent van Gogh 1853–1890

Caspar David Friedrich 1774–1840

Otto Dix 1891–1969

Paul Cézanne 1839–1906

1804 Napoleon crowns himself emperor of France ✹

1789–1799 French Revolution ✹

✹ 1841 Invention of paint tubes

| 1590 | 1630 | 1670 | 1710 | 1750 | 1790 | 1830 | 1870 | 1910 | 1950 | 1990 | 2030 |

Burning the Midnight Oil

"Oil on canvas" is probably the best known artistic technique of all, the epitome of a work of art. Oil paints allow artists to produce the greatest variety of colors and create the finest details in their pictures.

Oil paints consist of color pigments* and oil as a binder.* Artists use liquids called solvents, including turpentine, to make the paints wet so they can be applied to the canvas. Wet oil paint dries slowly, so an oil painter can often work on several paintings at the same time.

But before an artist can begin putting paint to canvas, he or she must first prepare the canvas with a primer.* Painters may also need to make preparatory studies, or small drawings that show the outlines of what the finished artwork should look like. The artist then makes underdrawings with charcoal, chalk, pencil, or watercolors on the canvas. Once the artist begins painting with oils, it's possible to put countless layers of paint on top of one another. But in doing so the painter has to follow the rule of "fat on lean," or placing thick layers over thin layers. Otherwise the paint can later crack or split. Because layering different colors of paint on top of one another creates unique effects, an artist can use several layers of oil paint or glazes* to create shades of color that can't be mixed on a palette.

Name:
  oil painting
Material:
  pigments,* linseed oil, poppy-seed oil, walnut oil, turpentine on canvas, wood, metal
Tools:
  palette, animal hair or soft bristle brush, rags
Some Artists:
  Jan van Eyck, Leonardo da Vinci, Caspar David Friedrich, Paul Cézanne, Vincent van Gogh, Otto Dix

The Adoration of the Magi (detail),
Leonardo da Vinci, 1481–82, oil on wood, Uffizi, Florence

The artist's method can be seen clearly in this unfinished painting by Italian artist Leonardo. The Old Masters built their oil paintings up layer by layer. The underdrawing was followed by an underpainting in neutral shades of gray, green, or brown. This process was done either with thin oil paint or with tempera paints, which were made of pigment,* oil, and water, and which dried more quickly.

Mount Sainte-Victoire,
Paul Cézanne,
c. 1897, oil on canvas,
Hermitage, St. Petersburg

Paul Cézanne was a
master of "alla prima"
painting. Here, the
canvas can be seen
shimmering through the
brushstrokes, and some
places are left completely
unpainted.

Painters used to make their own paints. The first tubes of paint were
invented in 1841, and they were very practical for painting outdoors.
Artists would place the paints on the canvas "alla prima," or without
any underpainting or glazes. Each portion of the painting was finished in one sitting. But sometimes a color was affected so strongly by
the adjacent colors that the artist had to alter it by mixing the colors
directly on the painting's surface. Or the painter might compose a painting out of tiny specks of color, starting with the lighter places and wor-
king towards the darker ones.

Today, there are no longer any strict rules for oil painting. Many painters prefer acrylic paints, which dissolve in water and dry much more
quickly than traditional paints. But acrylics cannot be used to make
paintings as finely layered as oils.

The Starry Night,
Vincent van Gogh, 1887, oil on canvas, Museum
of Modern Art, New York

Dutch artist Vincent van Gogh painted his pictures quickly.
He applied very thick layers of paint directly onto the
painting surface with rapid brushstrokes. This technique
is called impasto,* and it made Vincent's paintings very
expressive, giving them a strong feeling of movement.

Test your knowledge
"Alla prima" is an Italian
term. Can you guess what
the term means in Italian?
(Solution on page 46)

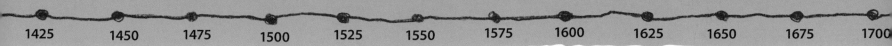

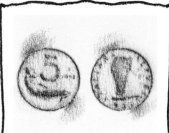

Name:
   semi-automatic
   techniques: frottage,
   grattage, décal-
   comanie
Material:
   paper, canvas,
   pencil, chalk, paint
Tools:
   wood panels,
   objects with raised
   structures, glass
   plates, tin cans,
   twine, brushes
Some Artists:
   George Sand,
   Max Ernst, Oscar
   Domínguez, Jackson
   Pollock

Only Chance Is Reliable

Brittany, 1925. A rainy vacation day at the shore. German painter Max Ernst sits in his room gazing at the wooden floor, amazed at the shapes he can discover in the wood grain. He gets a sheet of paper and a soft pencil, places the sheet on the floor, and makes a rubbing of the grainy shapes.

From that point on, "frottage" (from the French word *frotter*: to rub) became one of Max Ernst's favorite techniques. The shapes produced by the rubbings sparked his imagination. This was great for Ernst, who, as a Surrealist,* was interested in making puzzles out of everyday things. Strange flowers, petrified trees, never-before-seen insects … a whole natural history arose in his works. "Semi-automatic" is what the artist called his process, since he could only partially influence its course.

You can easily try out frottage yourself. A soft number 4A pencil, soft graphite stick,* or black crayon are best. You can find interesting shapes for rubbings almost anywhere!

Test your knowledge
Where can you find Max Ernst himself in this painting?
(Solution on page 46)

24

George Sand 1804–1876

Max Ernst 1891–1976
Oscar Domínguez 1906–1958
Jackson Pollock 1912–1956

1939–1945 Second World War ❋ 1941 Ernst flees the Nazis and settles in the United States

1922 Max Ernst relocates from Cologne to Paris ❋

❋ 1953 Ernst returns to France

| 1725 | 1750 | 1775 | 1800 | 1825 | 1850 | 1875 | 1900 | 1925 | 1950 | 1975 | 2000 |

Vox Angelica,
Max Ernst, 1943, oil on canvas, private collection

In this picture, composed of four panels pieced together, Max Ernst presents his techniques and artistic subjects almost as if they were part of a pattern book.

← **Decalcomania**

Nearly five hundred years before Max Ernst, Leonardo had mentioned that it was possible to throw a paint-soaked sponge against a wall and see any manner of things in the mark it left: "human heads, various animals, battles, reefs, seas, clouds, forests …" Ernst himself would spread liquid paint on a canvas, press a glass plate into it, and then remove the plate. He would then rework the individual forms in the plate's impression with a fine brush so that the viewer could also recognize them. This technique is called décalcomania: the transferring of an image onto another surface.

↑
Grattage

Max Ernst also used the rubbing technique in his paintings. He called this method "grattage," from the French verb *gratter*: to scratch. Ernst would apply paint to the canvas two or more times, then place it over a textured object and scrape over the topmost layer.

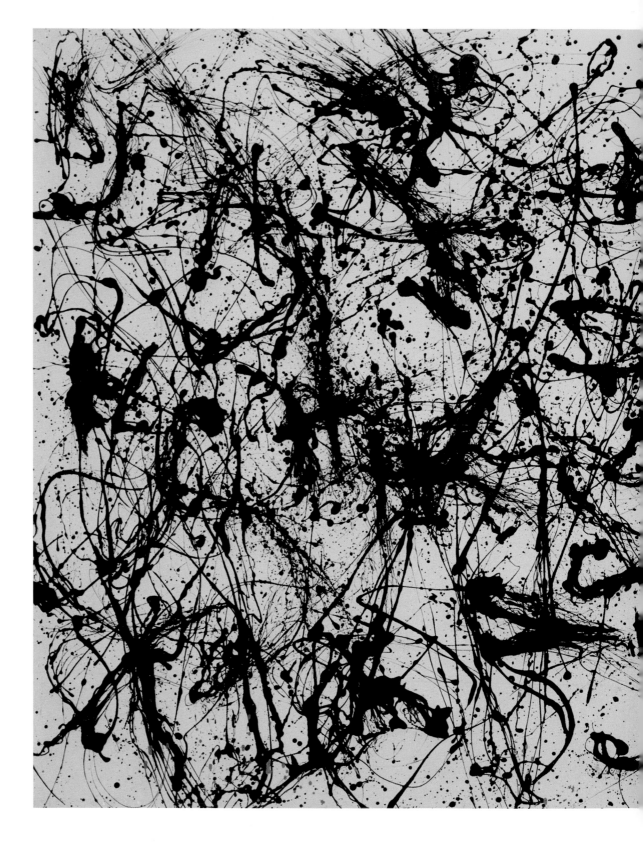

Max Ernst was always willing to experiment with unusual methods, and he encouraged others to do the same: "Tie an empty can to a piece of string one to two yards in length, drill a small hole in the bottom, and fill the can with paint. Swing the can back and forth over a flat canvas, using the movements of your arm, shoulder, and entire body to guide the can. In this way, amazing lines will drip onto the canvas."

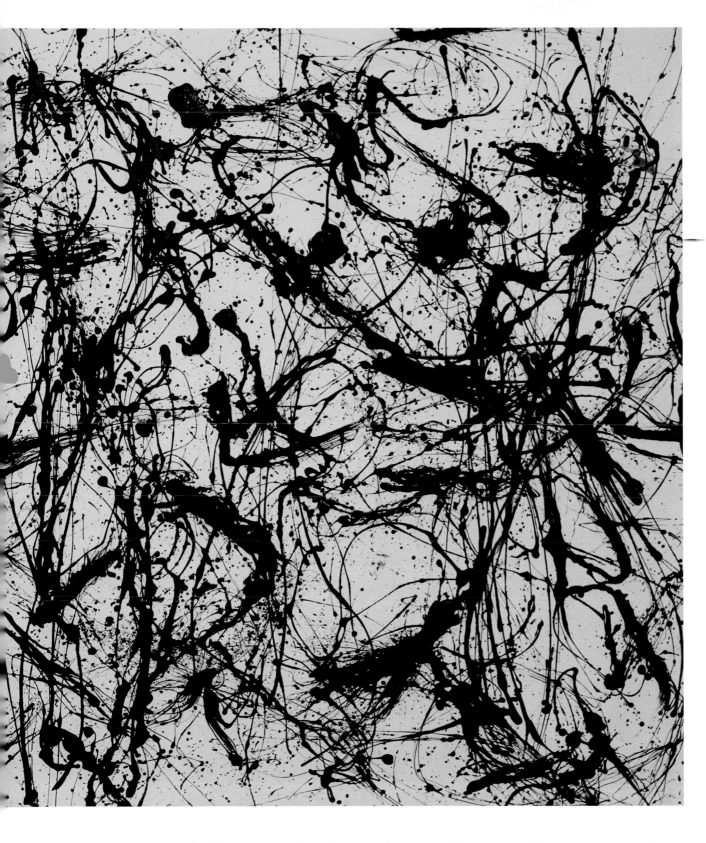

No. 32,
Jackson Pollock, 1950,
enamel on canvas,
Kunstsammlung
Nordrhein-Westfalen,
Düsseldorf

Jackson Pollock used his
whole body and a brush
and stick to drip and
shake the paint onto a
canvas lying flat on the
ground. Instead of thick
oil paints, he used thin
enamel paint for his "drip
paintings," with which
he sought to express his
inner self.

Ernst is said to have given this advice to the young American painter
Jackson Pollock, who developed the technique further and became world
famous for his drip paintings.

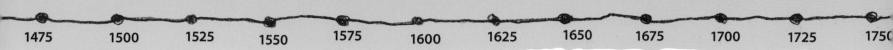

Name:
  modeling
Material:
  clay, plaster, wax,
  modeling clay
Tools:
  modeling tools,
  putty knife or trowel,
  sandpaper
Some Artists:
  Edgar Degas,
  Auguste Rodin

In Good Form

It's fun to build sand castles on the beach; to shape and create forms out of wet sand. But unfortunately these sculptures disappear with the next high tide.

Modeling is one of the techniques of sculpture. In contrast to carving, in which material is removed from a block, modeling involves adding or shaping materials—just like the building of a sand castle!

One material that is very easy to shape is clay, and it occurs naturally in the soil. When clay is fired in a special oven at over 2,300° F, it retains its shape. There are various kinds of clay, which can be identified by their color and their grog* content. Clay with low grog content is suited for smaller objects with fine details, while more grog gives stability to larger forms. Large sculptures also need an internal structure called a supporting framework, which prevents the artwork from falling apart. Modeling clay has to be kept moist during work. When the modeling is finished, the sculpture is hollowed out and allowed to dry slowly so that it does not crack during firing. Plaster and wax can also be used for modeling.

You too can try your hand at modeling a work of sculpture. But be sure not to use polyester resins, as their fumes are very poisonous. Instead, try using papier-mâché! You'll need old newspapers, a bucket, a stirring stick, wallpaper paste, and chicken wire. For painting your sculpture, you'll need a brush, white primer,* and your favorite paints.

Here's how: First, prepare the wallpaper paste in the bucket according to the directions, then tear the newspaper into small shreds and soak the shreds in the bucket. Bend the chicken wire into an enclosed shape and cover the shape with the shreds of paper. You can also soak larger pieces of newspaper in the paste and add them one at a time. Let your sculpture dry, cover it with a white layer of primer, and then paint it with any colors and designs you like.

28

Camille Claudel 1864–1943

Alberto Giacometti 1901–1966

Niki de St. Phalle 1930–2002

Louise Bourgeois 1911–2010

1961 Construction of the Berlin Wall

1989 Fall of the Berlin Wall

1775   1800   1825   1850   1875   1900   1925   1950   1975   2000   2025   2050

Elephant, Niki de St. Phalle, 1982–83, Stravinsky Fountain, Paris

Polyester resins, a type of plastic, are weather-resistant, strong, rugged, and lightweight—an ideal material for modeling large-scale sculptures. Polyester is often mixed with glass fibers to form another strong, lightweight material called fiberglass. This cheerful fiberglass elephant is part of a fountain at the Centre Georges Pompidou museum in Paris. It was designed by the French sculptor Niki de St. Phalle and her husband Jean Tinguely.

Auguste Rodin in his artist workshop in Meudon, surrounded by plaster fragments, 1902

French sculptor Rodin produced innumerable cast and clay models for his sculptures. This photo from the artist's workshop shows him between the cast models for his big bronze sculptures.

Test your knowledge
How many years did Rodin work on The Gates of Hell?
(Solution on page 46)

The Thinker,
Auguste Rodin, 1880–82, bronze, Musée Rodin, Paris

Rodin originally created The Thinker as the crowning element of his almost 23-foot-high bronze sculpture called The Gates of Hell. In 1880, the French government commissioned Rodin to design a gate for Paris's Museum of Decorative Arts. Rodin worked on the project until his death in 1917. The gate includes 186 human and animal figures, as well as fantastical creatures grouped around The Thinker in the middle. The Thinker was exhibited as an independent sculpture as early as 1888, and it has become one of Rodin's most famous works.

Here's one of the best ways to make sculptures in almost any kind of material: casting. This technique is often done at an art factory, or foundry. First, the caster covers the original work of art with sand, plaster, gelatin, clay, or silicon. When the original is removed, the impression on the inside of the covering corresponds to the outside of the original work. Then, a soft or liquid material (plaster, cement, or liquid clay or bronze) is pressed or poured into the empty covering. When this material dries or hardens, it forms a copy of the original artwork. Casting also takes place outside the art world. People even use it to make chocolate animals …

The Little Fourteen-Year-Old Dancer,
Edgar Degas, bronze and cotton, c. 1880, Musée d'Orsay, Paris

After Degas' death in 1917, over 150 sculptures were found in his studio. Only one of them, The Little Fourteen-Year-Old Dancer, had ever been exhibited. Degas used a variety of materials for his sculptures, including wax, clay, and textiles. He modeled his Dancer in wax and then supplied her with a bodice, tutu, ballet shoes, and real horse hair. After his death, 150 bronze casts were made of the work. They can be found today in several important museums.

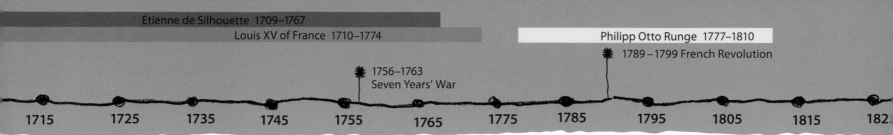

The Horse, the Rider, and the Clown,
Henri Matisse, 1947, color cutout, Herbert F. Johnson Museum of Art,
Cornell University, Ithaca, N.Y.

For a "positive image" the paper around the motif is cut away; for a
"negative image" the motif is cut out and the paper around it is left.
Henri Matisse used both methods at the same time with papers of
different colors, and he was able to achieve very sophisticated effects.

Paper cutouts function a bit
like a shadow theater. Shadows
on the wall can supply shapes
for your own paper cutouts.

Drawing with Scissors

How much can be expressed with a single line! A cutout artist can use paper to shape the outline of people, heads, animals, plants, and much more. And this silhouette* can reveal the most distinctive features of the person or object.

Thin paper can be cut easily with scissors. Thicker paper or cardboard might require the use of a paper-cutting knife. At the end of the 1700s, cutouts for decorating lamp shades or wallpaper were the latest rage.

Making silhouettes from the actual person was a popular pastime at social gatherings and parties. Silhouette makers can still be seen practicing their craft at fairs.

The French painter Henri Matisse discovered the art of making cutouts in the 1940s. He coined the expression "drawing with scissors." In recent years, contemporary artists have begun using this technique for images that can be many feet high and decorate entire rooms.

Name:
  cutouts
Material:
  white, black, or colored paper and cardboard
Tools:
  scissors, paper-cutting knife
Some Artists:
  Philipp Otto Runge, Henri Matisse, William Kentridge, Olaf Nicolai, Kara Walker

Dog Barking at the Moon, Philipp Otto Runge, white paper silhouette, blue paper, Hamburger Kunsthalle, Kupferstich-kabinett, Hamburg

In Runge's family, making silhouettes was a favorite pastime. Even the eleven-year-old Philipp mastered the art—without any pre-liminary drawing. Can't you almost hear the dog barking? Maybe you can even guess what breed it is?

	Pablo Picasso 1881–1973										
Georges Braque 1882–1963											
Hannah Höch 1889–1978											

1914–1918 First World War ☀
1908–1914 Picasso and Braque originate Cubism* ☀
1924 The Surrealist art movement officially begins ☀

| 1875 | 1880 | 1885 | 1890 | 1895 | 1900 | 1905 | 1910 | 1915 | 1920 | 1925 | 1930 |

Name:
  collage
Material:
  newspaper clippings, wallpaper, photographs, white and colored paper, cardboard, rope, fabric, glue
Tools:
  scissors
Some Artists:
  Pablo Picasso, Georges Braque, Max Ernst, Hannah Höch, Kurt Schwitters, Richard Hamilton, Jiří Kolář

Surprise Encounters

"Collage" comes from the French word *coller*: to glue. The choice of materials that can be used to make collages is almost endless.

It all began over a hundred years ago in Paris with an invention by two artist friends: a Spaniard named Pablo Picasso and a Frenchman named Georges Braque. Both men were looking for new ways to make art. They no longer wanted to depict real life in their paintings. Instead, they wanted their pictures to be new, independent realities in themselves! So they pasted objects onto their pictures to strengthen this effect of a special reality. Then, another Spanish artist in Paris named Juan Gris followed Picasso's and Braque's example. He added elements such as newspaper, bottle labels, and wallpaper to his artworks. Gris called these works "papiers collés," or "pasted papers."

Still Life with Chair Caning,
Pablo Picasso, 1912, oil and oilcloth on canvas, rope, Musée Picasso, Paris

This unusual picture is considered the first collage in the history of art. "Chair caning" is the name for a woven chair seat, but this "seat" is nothing other than a piece of patterned oilcloth. Picasso combined it with painted portions and surrounded the whole artwork with a rope.

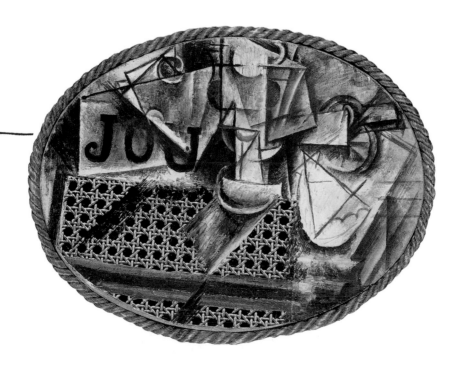

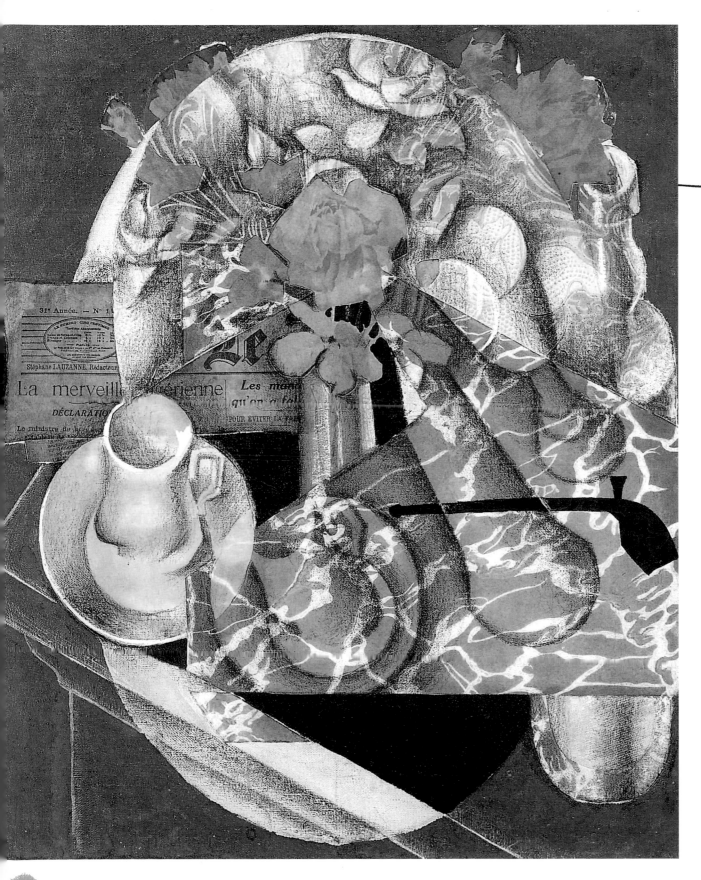

Flowers,
Juan Gris, 1914, oil,
collage, and pencil
on canvas, Hester
Diamond Collection

Juan Gris followed
Picasso's and Braque's
example of brown tones
and black-and-white
contrasts only for a short
time. His collages soon
included vividly color-
ful objects, such as the
bright flowers on this
coffee table set.

After the First World War, the most destructive war in human history at the time, young artists proclaimed a revolution. The time for pretty pictures made with delicate oil paint was over. Instead, the fractured, complicated nature of collage technique—and its use of "ugly" everyday objects and litter—better mirrored the turmoil of the times. This technique helped inspire a new art movement called Dada.*

Then a few years later, people began talking about another art movement called Surrealism.* The prefix *sur* is French for "over." Surrealist artists were interested in the secrets that could be found beyond everyday reality, in the dreams and other "subconscious" thoughts of the human mind. They used collage to put objects together that normally had nothing to do with each other—a technique that led to surprising and puzzling new images.

The principle of collage, the combining of fragments and ideas in strange ways, was also used in literature and music.

In addition to Unsatisfeedle, Hannah Höch's picture book contains a whole variety of other fabulous creatures such as the "Loftylara," the "Runfasts," the "Snifti," and "Longfringes." Maybe you'd also like to invent some of your own fantastical creatures with scissors and glue?

Unsatisfeedle,
Hannah Höch, 1945, collage, Berlinische Galerie, Berlin

Hannah Höch was one of Berlin's Dada* artists. Thirty years after the founding of the art movement, and after a second enormous war had shaken the world, she composed a children's book with collages and poems. Look closely: can you figure out what she used to create the mischievous "Unsatisfeedle" character from her book?

Further reading:
You can find ideas and inspiration for making your own collages in *Look at Me: Portraits for Children* by Claudia Strand, Prestel Verlag, 2012.

Pablo Picasso 1881–1973
Jean Dubuffet 1901–1989
Joseph Cornell 1903–1972
Robert Rauschenberg 1925–2008

1912 Pablo Picasso creates sculptures using found objects | 1914–1918 First World War | 1930 Daniel Spoerri is born | 1939–1945 Second World War

1895   1900   1905   1910   1915   1920   1925   1930   1935   1940   1945   1950

Name:
  assemblage
Material:
  everyday objects of every sort, pieces of wood, metal, plants, stones
Tools:
  hammer, screwdriver, saw
Some Artists:
  Pablo Picasso, Jean Dubuffet, Joseph Cornell, Daniel Spoerri, Arman, Robert Rauschenberg, Christo and Jeanne-Claude

Finders Keepers

Do you like collecting things? Special stones or pieces of wood? Marbles, feathers, or toys? Many professional artists also make works of art out of the things they find.

The name of this technique, "assemblage," comes from French and means "assortment" or "composition." It was invented in the 1900s as artists began to develop new methods that went beyond traditional materials and techniques. In contrast to a collage, which is usually made up of flat materials, an assemblage is three-dimensional. But like a collage, an assemblage can also combine things that aren't usually related in the everyday world. In this way assemblages can pose riddles and tell stories.

There are even artworks that combine painting and assemblage. American artist Robert Rauschenberg created a sensation at the beginning of the 1950s when he attached everyday objects onto his paintings, sometimes even painting on the objects as well. The European artist couple Christo and Jeanne-Claude further developed assemblage into the art of wrapping buildings, objects, and things in nature.

Create your own assemblage out of objects that inspire you. Maybe you can think up a story to go along with them ...

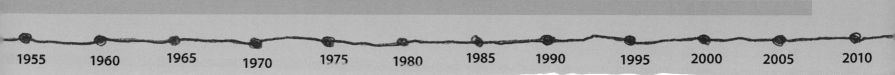

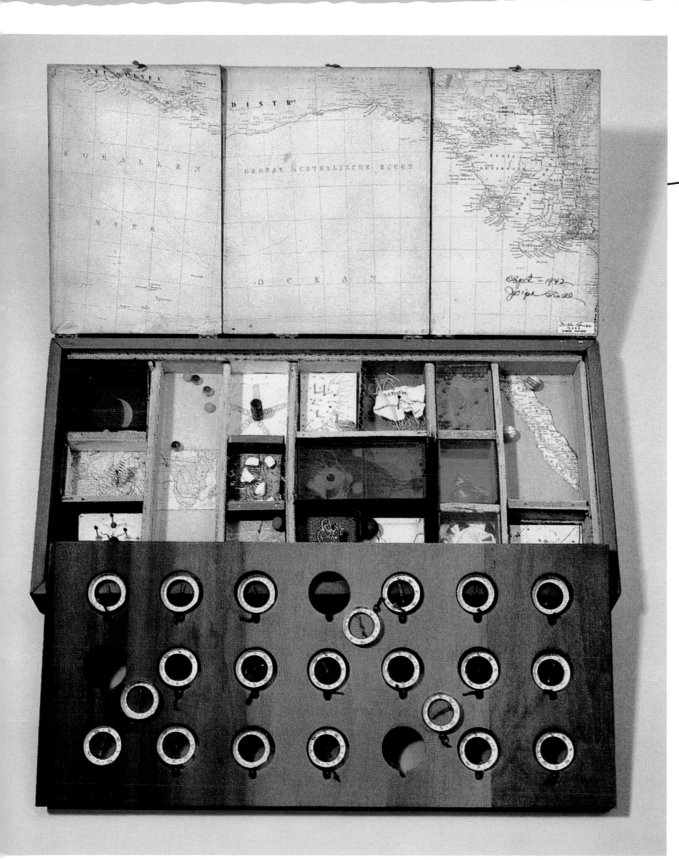

Object (Roses des Vents), Joseph Cornell, 1942–53, assemblage, The Museum of Modern Art, New York

"Roses des Vents" is French for "wind roses." A wind rose is found on a compass and represents the directions of the wind. Joseph Cornell incorporated twenty-one compasses in this work. Beneath them are more compartments containing objects and pictures that remind people of traveling. These objects are in keeping with the maps of the Australian coastlines, with which the artist lined the cover of the box.

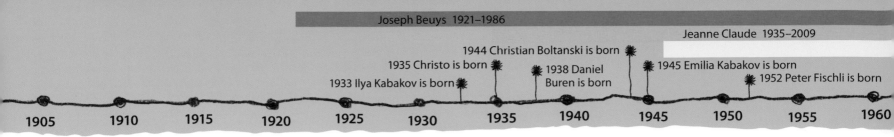

Joseph Beuys 1921–1986

Jeanne Claude 1935–2009

1944 Christian Boltanski is born

1935 Christo is born

1933 Ilya Kabakov is born

1938 Daniel Buren is born

1945 Emilia Kabakov is born

1952 Peter Fischli is born

1905 1910 1915 1920 1925 1930 1935 1940 1945 1950 1955 1960

Name:
installation
Material:
spaces, objects, any kind of material, light, sounds, music
Tools:
anything necessary for building the installation, including a giant crane
Some Artists:
Joseph Beuys, Daniel Buren, Peter Fischli and David Weiss, Christo and Jeanne-Claude, Ilya and Emilia Kabakov, Gregor Schneider

Art Takes on Space

An entire palace as a work of art! In 2012 the French artist Daniel Buren created an enormous installation in the Grand Palais in Paris. It covered around 145,000 square feet.

An artist can use any conceivable material for an installation, including temporary ones like light and sound. He can even consider the visitors moving through the work of art as part of his creation. Installations are meant to change the way we experience space. They are often designed for specific locations, with which they are closely connected. An installation can only be shown "in situ," or in the specific site for which it is designed.

Daniel Buren's title refers to this idea: "Travail in Situ," which can be translated as "work in situ." He worked with the light falling through the giant glass dome and the great windows of the Grand Palais. The light entering the space activated the colored foils attached to the window panes, and it illuminated the colored discs that Buren had installed in the space like umbrellas. The visitor is bathed in a sea of color. The exhibition lasted for six weeks and then everything was dismantled.

Installations can also be made outdoors, in "exterior spaces." They don't always have to be as large as the work by Daniel Buren. The name for this kind of art was coined in the late 1970s, as artists increasingly experimented with unusual materials, using them to create spaces. Installation art has changed people's ideas about what "sculpture" or other three-dimensional art can be.

Did you know?
The Grand Palais was build for the Paris World's Fair* in 1900.

40

Excentrique(s) – Travail in Situ,
Daniel Buren, installation, 9 May–21 June, 2012, Grand Palais, Paris

The largest glass roof in Europe arches over the roof of the Grand Palais. Buren's plastic discs cast brilliant colors onto the floor and merge into new tones: a festival of color and light. Loudspeakers softly repeat the names of the colors in thirty-seven languages.

Template,
Ai WeiWei, 2007, doors
and windows from
traditional buildings
from the Ming and Qing
dynasties (1368–1911),
Documenta Kassel

For the world art exhibition Documenta 12 in Kassel, Germany, the Chinese artist Ai Weiwei constructed a 26-foot-high temple pavilion of 1,001 doors and windows. Four days after the exhibition opened, Template collapsed during a storm. But Ai Weiwei did not consider this a disaster. He saw the collapse as the creation of a new sculpture, one that documented the forces of nature. He also felt the collapse would remind viewers that the doors and windows from which Template was made had come from demolished houses in China. These traditional buildings from the Ming and Qing dynasties (1368–1911) had been destroyed to make way for modern new buildings.

Glossary

ABSTRACT In art, the term abstract refers to colors and forms that don't resemble real objects.

ALLIES During the First and Second World Wars, the Allies were a group of countries led by the United States and the United Kingdom that fought against another group of countries led by Germany.

ANGELIC SALUTATION In Christianity, this term refers to the greeting of the angel Gabriel to Mary as he announced that she would give birth to Jesus Christ.

BINDER is a neutrally-colored material that helps paint stick to a canvas or other surface.

BYZANTINES were inhabitants of an early Christian empire also known as the Eastern Roman Empire, which had its capitol at Constantinople (present-day Istanbul).

CUBISM In Cubism, objects and figures are broken up into geometric forms and shown from several angles at once: from the front, from the side, from behind and below. Pablo Picasso and his friend and fellow artist

Georges Braque originated Cubism around 1908, igniting an artistic revolution in the process.

DADA was a movement of artists and writers founded in Zurich in 1916, which soon spread to Berlin, Cologne, Hannover, Paris, and New York. The name originated when one of the movement's founders randomly stuck a knife into a French dictionary. The knife pointed at the word *dada*, French for "hobby horse."

FIXATIVE is a transparent substance that is sprayed on a picture to protect its surface.

GESSO, a type of surface on which painters create works of art, consists of plaster or chalk and glue.

GLAZE is a paint applied in a thin and transparent layer.

GOLD LEAF, SILVER LEAF refers to gold or silver that has been hammered into extremely thin sheets.

GRAPHITE is a mineral often used in artist pencils.

GROG is fired, finely ground clay.

GUM ARABIC is a sticky tree sap.

HATCHING involves drawing many fine, straight lines parallel to one another or crossing each other (crosshatching).

IRON OXIDE is a kind of rust.

IMPASTO, which refers to thickly applied paint, comes from the Italian word pasta, meaning dough.

JAPANESE PAPER (WASHI) is handmade paper from Japan, made from the fibers of specific shrubs.

LAID PAPER is paper with a ribbed texture.

LAPIS LAZULI is a semi-precious stone still used today to produce the highest quality ultramarine blue. The name ultramarine comes from the Latin word *ultramarinus*, or "beyond the sea," a reference to the fact that lapis lazuli was imported to Europe from distant lands east of the Mediterranean Sea.

LEAD ORE is lead-containing stone.

LIMEWASH is lime mineral that has been thinned by being soaked in water.

MUSES are ancient Greek goddesses of the arts.

ORNAMENT is a decorative pattern.

PIGMENT is a material that gives something color. Pigments used to be derived from natural substances such as soil or plant and animal matter. In the 1800s, there was pigment called "mummy

brown," which was made from real Egyptian mummies. Today many pigments are made synthetically.

POMPEII was a city in southern Italy beneath the volcano Mount Vesuvius. In 80 B.C., ancient Pompeii became a Roman colony and many wealthy Romans settled there. During the eruption of Vesuvius in A.D. 79, the city was buried by pumice, ash, and molten lava within a few hours. The ancient city remained largely preserved beneath its deep layer of ash and debris. The excavation of Pompeii began in the middle of the 1700s.

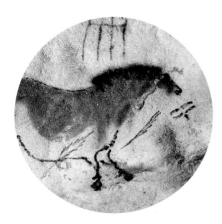

PREHISTORIC means before recorded history, from the earliest period that humans inhabited the Earth.

PRIMER is a material that artists use on canvases and sculptures. Primers create a surface on which a work of art can be painted.

RENAISSANCE This word comes from a French term for "rebirth." During the Renaissance, which lasted from the first half of the 1400s until about 1600, artists and scholars in Europe rediscovered the achievements of the ancient Greeks and Romans. People also investigated how things and processes in the real world actually worked.

SILHOUETTE is a picture that shows the outline of a person or object in shadow. This type of art was named after the French finance minister Étienne de Silhouette (1709–1767). It was said that he was so stingy, he decorated his castle with silhouettes because they were cheaper than paintings.

SINOPIA are preparatory drawings named for the Turkish city of Sinop, from where the red earth color used in those drawings was imported.

STANDING PRESS is a press in which a wheel is used to lower the printing plate from above and exert the pressure vertically.

SUMERIANS were an ancient people in southern Mesopotamia (present-day Iraq).

SURREALISM The Surrealists were interested in everything that went beyond reality—the French word *sur* means "beyond." The term was coined in 1917, and in the 1920s and 1930s Surrealist artists and writers created quite a stir. Familiar things were made to seem strange and were combined into surprising and novel images—like in a dream. For the Surrealists, the marvelous, mysterious, and fantastic were just as true as the real.

VELLUM is a paper-like material made of animal skin, on which artists used to paint and draw.

WARSAW PACT was a pact of alliance under the leadership of the Soviet Union, signed in Warsaw on May 14, 1955 by Albania, Bulgaria, East Germany, Poland, Romania, Czechoslovakia, Hungary, and the Soviet Union.

WORLD'S FAIR is an international exhibition in which the participating countries display their achievements in technology, industry, and the arts and crafts.

Answers to the quiz questions:

page 5:   Silver is very expensive.

page 23:   In Italian, "Alla prima" means "at once."
             This first layer of a painting has to be made just right.

page 24:   At the picture's lower right, Ernst depicted a group of drawing
             instruments called compasses that form his first name: MAX.

page 30:   Rodin worked on his Gates of Hell
             for a total of thirty-seven years.

© 2013, 9th printing 2021
Prestel Verlag,
Munich · London · New York
A member of Penguin Random House
Verlagsgruppe GmbH
Neumarkter Strasse 28 · 81673 Munich

Front cover:
Katsushiha Hokusai (p. 14) Van Gogh (p. 23)
Niki de St. Phalle (p. 29)

Frontispiece: Giovanni Battista Tiepolo,
ceiling fresco of the staircase (detail), 1750–53,
Würzburg Residenz

Photo credits: Artothek: p. 4, Alinari – Artothek: p. 7,
Blauel/Gnamm – Artothek: p. 19, Hans Hinz – Artothek:
p. 18, Peter Willi – Artothek: p. 22, akg-images / Ma-
nuel Cohen: p. 10, akg-images: p. 25, p. 26/27, Natalia
Ivanova/Allpix/laif: p. 41, Adam Berry/Bloomberg via
Getty Images: p. 42/43, Jacek Bogdan: p. 28, Giovanni
Dall'Orto: p. 12, Peter Stepan: p. 29, Daniel Stockman:
p. 30, Frontispiece: Wolf-Christian von der Mülbe

Library of Congress Control Number: 2016937533
A CIP catalogue record for this book is available from
the British Library.

Translation: Cynthia Hall
Copyediting: Brad Finger
Image editing: Sabine Tauber
Design: Michael Schmölzl,
agenten.und.freunde, Munich
Art direction: Cilly Klotz
Layout: Meike Sellier
Production management: Astrid Wedemeyer,
Matthias Korff
Separations: ReproLine Mediateam, Munich
Printing and binding: Printer Trento, Trento

Penguin Random House Verlagsgruppe FSC®N001967

Prestel Publishing compensates the CO_2 emissions
produced from the making of this book by supporting
a reforestation project in Brazil. Find further information
on the project here:
www.ClimatePartner.com/14044-1912-1001

Printed in Italy
ISBN 978-3-7913-7136-8

www.prestel.com